KU-633-173

RHS

Outdoor Adventure Handbook

Ideas and activities for exploring outside!

■SCHOLASTIC

Contents

Let's Go Outside

This book is packed with amazing outdoor adventures, big and small. From identifying trees, to tracking wildlife and even growing your own incredible plants, there are lots of wild ideas for having fun outside. You can do some of the activities in a back garden or local park, and some will take you further afield.

Outdoor adventure checklist

Have a backpack of useful things to hand so you're ready for an outdoor adventure, whatever the weather. You should have:

- [x] sun hat
- [x] sun cream
- [x] waterproof jacket
- [x] water bottle
- [ ] sturdy shoes
- [ ] notebook
- [ ] pens and pencils
- [ ] snack
- [ ] first aid kit
- [ ] torch
- [ ] compass

Stay Safe

Taking risks and overcoming challenges is an important part of being an outdoor adventurer, but it's even more important to look after yourself! Follow these safety tips when you're out and about.

Look after yourself

- Make sure you're with a grown-up whenever you are taking part in riskier activities, like climbing trees.

- Take extra care when exploring around water and keep an eye on younger brother and sisters.

- Wash your hands after going outside, this is especially important if you have touched soil or stagnant water. Use soap and warm water, and scrub for at least twenty seconds.

Look after nature

- Always leave wild areas exactly as you found them. Take all your belongings and litter home.

- Make sure you have permission to pick flowers or other plants in an area before you do so, and only take a little so as not to damage the plant.

- Keep an eye out for wildlife homes, like nests and burrows, and be particularly careful around them.

Look out for more safety tips throughout the book.

- Only use sharp tools like scissors if you have been given permission by a grown-up and know how to use them safely. If an activity requires a knife, make sure there is a grown-up there to help.

- Drink plenty of water, particularly if it's hot, even if you don't feel thirsty.

- Cover up and wear sunhats and sunblock if it's sunny to avoid burning or getting heatstroke.

- Let a grown-up know if you injure yourself or get bitten or stung.

- Never collect mushrooms, berries or plants to eat as they may be poisonous.

Spring Checklist

In spring, as the weather warms up and the days grow longer, gardens and parks begin bursting back to life! Which of these spring signs can you spot? Tick the boxes when you see them on your outdoor adventures.

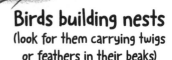

Birds building nests
(look for them carrying twigs or feathers in their beaks)

☐

Blossom on trees

☐

Leaf buds appearing

☐

Ducklings, cygnets or goslings in ponds and lakes

☐

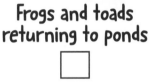

Daffodils, tulips,
or crocuses blooming
☐

Frogs and toads
returning to ponds
☐

Butterflies, bees and
hoverflies visiting flowers
☐

Bluebells and wild garlic
in the woods
☐

Even if you don't
spot ramson (wild
garlic), you might catch a
whiff of it! With bright green
leaves and white, star-like
flowers, this strong-scented
plant is a smelly sign
of spring.

11

Tree Guide

Trees remind us of the power of nature with their amazing transformation from tiny seeds into mighty plants. It's easiest to identify trees in spring and summer, when their branches are thick with glossy leaves. Discover how to tell one towering tree from the next with this handy guide.

The round leaves of the aspen flutter in even the smallest breeze, giving the tree its nickname 'quaking aspen'.

Beech

Height: up to 40 metres (13

Type: deciduous

Range: Central Europe

Horse Chestnut

Height: up to 40 metres (132 feet)

Type: deciduous

Range: South East Europe

Blackthorn

Height: up to 7 metr (23 feet)

Type: deciduous

Range: Europe

Silver Birch

Height: up to 30 metres (98 feet)

Type: deciduous

Range: Europe, Central Asia

Cedar

Height: up to 35 metres (115 feet)

Type: evergreen

Range: North Africa, West Asia

Sweet Cherry

Height: up to 9 metres (29 feet)

Type: deciduous

Range: Europe, Asia

Hazel

Height: up to 12 metres (39 feet)

Type: deciduous

Range: Europe, North Africa, West Asia

After being pollinated by insects, the flowers of the sweet cherry tree grow into deep-red fruits.

Douglas Fir

Height: up to 55 metres (180 feet)

Type: evergreen

Range: North America, Central America

Field Maple

Height: up to 20 metres (66 feet)

Type: deciduous

Range: Europe,
West Asia

Monkey Puzzle

Height: up to 30 metres (98 feet)

Type: evergreen

Range: South America

This ancient species of tree has been around since dinosaurs walked the Earth. Its spiky leaves wind in a spiral around its branches.

English Oak

Height: up to 40 metres (132 feet)

Type: deciduous

Range: Europe

Scots Pine

Height: up to 35 metres (115 feet)

Type: evergreen

Range: Europe, Asia

Sycamore

Height: up to 35 metres (115 feet)

Type: deciduous

Range: Europe, West Asia

White Willow

Height: up to 25 metres (82 feet)

Type: deciduous

Range: Europe, Asia

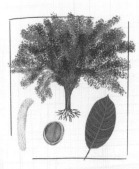

Walnut

Height: up to 35 metres (115 feet)

Type: deciduous

Range: Europe, Central Asia

Yew

Height: up to 20 metres (66 feet)

Type: evergreen

Range: Europe, North West Africa, South West Asia

How to Climb a Tree

Scrambling over branches and shimmying up trunks takes skill and daring, but the sense of achievement once a tree has been conquered is worth it! Here are some tips for picking which trees are best to climb and how to do it safely.

Get ready

- Make sure there is a grown-up with you at all times. Show them these tips so they can help you find the perfect climbing tree.

- Choose trainers or boots with good grip and clothes you can move in easily.

Find your tree

- Look for a tree with a thick trunk and branches at least twice as thick as your leg.

- Don't climb trees with rotting or dead branches, and avoid trees with bird's nests.

Start climbing

- Make sure three limbs (hands or feet) are touching the tree at all times. For example, you could have two feet and one hand on one branch, while your other hand reaches for the next branch.

- Taking measured risks is great, but if you're not having fun, or you don't think you can reach the next branch safely, then you should stop straight away.

- In most cases, you won't be able to get to the 'top' of the tree, as the branches will become too thin. Once you've reached a spot you're comfortable with, have a look at what you can see from there before climbing back down the way you came up.

Always ask an adult for permission before going outside.

17

Going Camping

Whether you head out to the wilderness
or pitch up in your own back garden, a camping trip is
one of the most exciting outdoor adventures you can go on!

Pick a suitable site

To find the perfect place to pitch your tent, look for a piece of flat, dry
ground. If you're out in the countryside, stay away from streams and rivers,
and avoid setting up camp at the bottom of a hill.

Put up your tent

Tents come in all sorts of shapes and sizes, so make sure you read
the instructions a couple of times before attempting to put it up.
If it's windy, pitch your tent so the opening is facing away from
the incoming wind.

Store food securely

Stop wildlife or creepy crawlies munching your
snacks, by keeping them in sealed containers.

Camping Games

No trip is complete without some great games! Here are a few to try out on your next camping adventure.

Wink, murder

Pick someone to be the 'detective' and send them out of earshot for a moment. The rest of the group stands in a circle and agrees on someone to be the 'murderer'. The detective comes back and heads to the middle of the circle, while the murderer begins 'killing' people by winking at them. When a player is killed, they should act out a dramatic death, then sit on the ground. The detective gets three chances to guess who the murderer is. If they guess correctly, the murderer becomes the detective for the next round. If they fail, they stay on as the detective for another go.

Sleeping bag race

Use some sticks to mark a start and finish line – make sure the area is free of litter, potholes or big rocks. At the start line, climb into your sleeping bags and ask someone who isn't racing to give you a countdown from three, before shouting "Go!" Hop as fast as you can to the finish line – the first person across it wins!

Capture the flag

Capture the flag is a fun game for a larger group, especially if you love to run. The only supplies you need for the game are two flags (you could use jumpers). Divide your group into two teams and designate an area for each. Give the teams time to hide their flags, then each team searches for the other flag. If you get caught in the other team's territory, you go to 'jail' until a teammate can rescue you (without getting caught too). The first team to capture the other team's flag is the winner.

Hide and seek

Hide and seek is a fun game to play at a campsite because there are many more places to hide than at home. Before you take off and hide, make sure you set up ground rules to keep everyone safe. That might include setting boundaries for the play area or determining how long the seeker should count before coming to find everyone. For a fun variation, try roving hide and seek. While on a hike, the hider runs ahead and hides while the rest of the group keeps walking. Whoever finds them first gets to hide next.

Always ask an adult for permission before going out to play.

21

Wild Water Games

Water fights are a splash-tastic way to cool down on summer days. It's important not to waste water though – in hot, dry periods be responsible and avoid using garden hoses.

Soaking sponges

Using a bucket of water and some washing up sponges, create D.I.Y. water bombs and have fun racing around the garden soaking each other! Split into two teams and score points for a hit (though avoid throwing sponges at your friends' heads). Choose a 'safe spot' for each team – players can wait here without being water-bombed if they want a break.

Duck, duck, splash!

Everyone sits in a circle, apart from one person who is the splasher. The splasher walks around the circle, carrying a cup filled with water, tapping each player on the head and saying "Duck!" After a few taps, instead of saying "Duck!" the splasher pours the cup of water over another player's head! The player must get up and chase the splasher around the circle, trying to catch them before the splasher sits in their spot. If the splasher makes it back, the player that got splashed takes over their role.

Soaking sponges

Split into two teams and sit in a line on the grass. Each team needs a sponge, a bucket full of water at the front of the line, and an empty bucket at the back. On "Go!" the player at the front of the line must soak the sponge in the bucket of water and pass it over their head to the next person in the line. When the sponge reaches the back of the line, the player at the back squeezes as much water as possible into the empty bucket, before running to the front of the line and beginning again. After three minutes, the team with the most water in their bucket wins!

Rockin' towers

If your campsite is near a river or beach that has a lot of smooth stones, you could try building rock towers. Challenge your friends to build tall towers from the pebbles or stones you find and see what you can come up with. Turn it into a game to see who can create the tallest tower or the one with the most rocks included. You should always ask permission before collecting stones, as some natural areas may have rules against moving rocks. It is very important that you take extra care when you are near the water, especially as some surfaces may be uneven.

Be careful when playing with water. A grown-up should supervise these activities.

How to

Read a Map

Maps are amazing – they give lots of information about the area around you, show you the most direct route from one place to another and help you find your way if you get lost.

A map is normally divided into grid boxes to help you pinpoint an exact location and everything is shrunk down to scale. This means that, though everything is much smaller on a map than it is in real life, it's all in proportion. For example, one hundred metres in real life might be one centimetre on a map. A scale is shown like this:

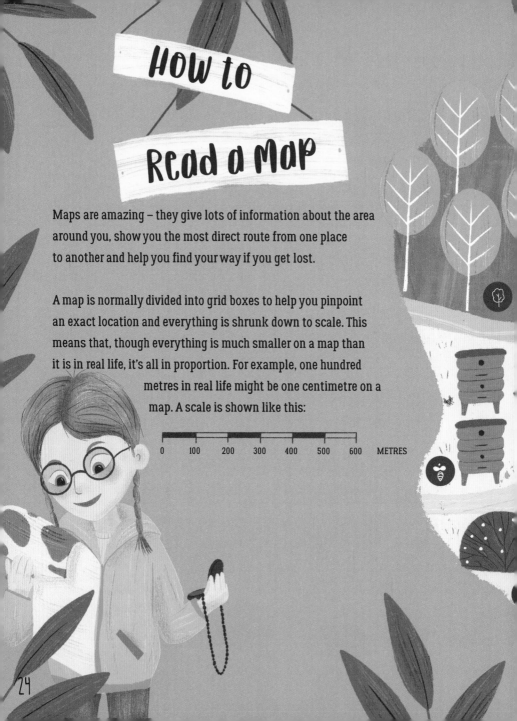

| 0 | 100 | 200 | 300 | 400 | 500 | 600 | METRES |

Key

A key shows what the symbols on a map mean. Can you find the beehive, bird hide and pond on this garden map?

- river
- path
- bench
- evergreen tree
- deciduous tree
- flowerbed
- pond
- beehive
- bird hide
- hedge

Draw a Garden Map

Get your pens and pencils ready – it's time to create a garden map of your own! You could draw a map of your back garden if you have one, or use your imagination to come up with a dream outdoor space.

Key

Copy the symbols from the previous page or come up with your own.

☐	_____	☐	_____
☐	_____	☐	_____
☐	_____	☐	_____
☐	_____	☐	_____
☐	_____	☐	_____

0   100   200   300   400   500   600   METRES

Build a Tepee

Tepees are simple shelters that are easy to build, indoors or outdoors. They make excellent dens for reading books, daydreaming or keeping an eye out for garden wildlife.

You will need:

- six sticks, around 1.5 metres long (bamboo or dowel works well)
- rope, around 1 metre
- 15–20 clothes pegs
- an old sheet
- cosy cushions and blankets (optional)
- fairy lights (optional)

1. Gather the top of the sticks in one hand and use the other hand to wrap the rope around. Wind it over and under each of the sticks, pulling them together tightly as you go. Secure with a knot.

2. Lift the sticks up, so they are standing vertically, and spread them out into a cone shape to form a circle with an open front. If you're building your tepee outside, then push all six sticks a few centimetres into the ground.

3. Wrap the sheet around the sticks, lining up the edges with the tepee's opening. Pin the sheet together at the top using pegs, then peg the bottom edges of the sheet to the base of the two front sticks.

4. Add a peg to each of the sticks at the top and bottom, securing the sheet in place and tucking the extra fabric under.

5. Throw in some cushions, blankets and fairy lights if you like, and cosy up inside your secret den!

Make a Wilderness Compass

An outdoor adventurer should always carry a compass, but if you forget to pack it, you can find your way through the wilderness with this basic D.I.Y. version.

You will need:

- a needle
- a leaf
- a magnet

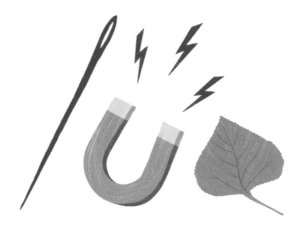

Be careful when using a needle. A grown-up should supervise this activity.

1. Rub the needle over the magnet around fifty times to magnetise it. Stroke it repeatedly in the same direction, rather than back and forth.

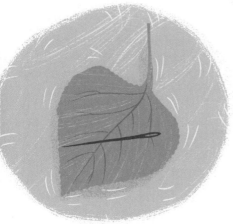

2. Pick a flat leaf and balance the needle on top of it. You could try floating the leaf on some still water.

3. If no wind is allowed to hit the leaf, the needle should pull the floating leaf clockwise or counter-clockwise to orient itself north-south.

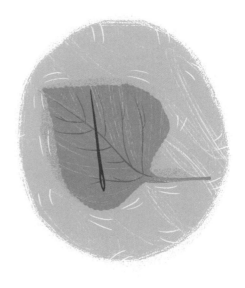

If you don't have a magnet, you can use wool from your clothes, or even some of your hair, to rub on the needle to magnetise it using static electricity.

Make a  Sundial Clock

Use the sun to tell the time with this simple clock. You're likely to have all the bits and bobs you need to make it lying around the house.

You will need:

a watch, clock or phone
(to check the time against)

a paper straw, or recycled plastic straw

A paper plate

stones or push pins

Make your sundial clock on a sunny, cloudless day in summer. Get everything ready at 11.30, so you can begin at 12 o'clock!

a compass

a ruler

crayons

a sharp pencil

1. Write the number 12 at the very edge of your plate. Push your pencil through the centre of the plate, then pull it out so you are left with a hole in the middle. Using your ruler, draw a line from the hole to the number 12.

2. Stick a straw into the hole. If you are in the Northern Hemisphere, use a compass to work out which way is North, and push the straw so it slants slightly towards it. If you are in the Southern Hemisphere, slant your straw towards South.

3. At exactly 12 o'clock, rotate the plate so the straw's shadow is aligned with the line you drew. Secure your plate with stones or pins, so that it doesn't move position or get blown away.

4. At exactly 1 o'clock, return to the plate and write the number 1 at the edge, where the shadow is now falling.

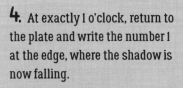

5. Repeat this process until dusk, marking every hour, until your sundial is complete. Don't worry if the lines you draw don't look like a clock face.

The next time it's sunny, see if you can now tell the time without the help of your watch.

Make a Kite

Follow these seven simple steps to create a colourful kite to take to the skies on windy days.

You will need:

- a white bin liner or other large recycled plastic bag
- two pieces of wooden dowel, or two sticks, 30 cm and 40 cm
- strong sticky tape or parcel tape
- kite string, or alternative strong, thin string
- permanent markers
- ribbon or tissue paper (optional)

Ask a grown-up to help you with this activity.

1. Open the bin liner or plastic bag and cut across the top to remove the handles. Cut down each of the sides so you have two rectangular pieces of plastic. Put one to the side for now (you could use it to make another kite later!).

2. Lay the dowel or sticks in a cross shape on top of the plastic, with the longer piece running vertically and the shorter piece running horizontally across it, about two thirds of the way up.

Do not play with plastic bags, and never put one over your head.

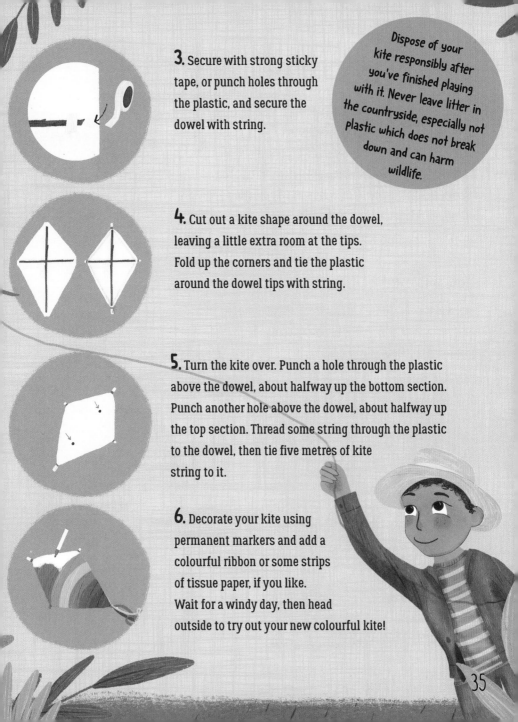

3. Secure with strong sticky tape, or punch holes through the plastic, and secure the dowel with string.

Dispose of your kite responsibly after you've finished playing with it. Never leave litter in the countryside, especially not plastic which does not break down and can harm wildlife.

4. Cut out a kite shape around the dowel, leaving a little extra room at the tips. Fold up the corners and tie the plastic around the dowel tips with string.

5. Turn the kite over. Punch a hole through the plastic above the dowel, about halfway up the bottom section. Punch another hole above the dowel, about halfway up the top section. Thread some string through the plastic to the dowel, then tie five metres of kite string to it.

6. Decorate your kite using permanent markers and add a colourful ribbon or some strips of tissue paper, if you like. Wait for a windy day, then head outside to try out your new colourful kite!

35

Nature's Music

Birds singing, wind whistling, rain pattering – nature makes its own special music! Join in its song by creating your own instruments from natural materials.

Wash your hand after collecting objects outside to av spreading germs.

Grass whistle

You will need:

- a piece of grass

1. Put your thumbs together with a blade of grass between them, stretched so it is taut.

2. Blow through the gap, so the air flows over the grass.

3. Adjust the piece of grass until you hear a high-pitched whistling sound!

36

Tambourine stick

You will need:

- a stick with a fork in it
- string or wire
- a few shells with holes in them

Ask an adult to help you with this activity.

1. Thread the string through the shells.

2. Tie the string around the two prongs of the forked stick.

3. Snip the ends of the string, then shake, rattle and roll!

35

Sunrise Stroll

The early bird catches the worm – but the early adventurer hears the best birdsong! Set out on a walk before sunrise and listen out for the dawn chorus of tweets, chirrups and chirps.

Wear warm clothes, co
footwear and pack som
tasty breakfast.

me of the earliest birds
start singing are song
rushes, blackbirds and
bins.

Make
sure you take
an adult with you if
u're heading further
than your back
garden.

Male birds tend to do most of the singing. They sing for two reasons – to attract female birds and to mark out their territories.

Wherever you are in the world, there are different birds to watch, all year round.

ch to July is the best time to
birds sing. In May, you might
returning migrating birds
uding warblers and nightingales!

What birds
did you spot?
Use the guide on
pages 48-51 to help
identify them!

Star Spotting

Shapes in the stars are called constellations – some are easier to spot than others! If you look up at the sky on a clear summer's night, you should be able see some of the starry patterns on these pages.

On very clear, dark summer nights, you might be able to spot our galaxy – the Milky Way. It appears like a bright band across the sky but is actually a flat spiral.

Ursa Major

Ursa Mi

Cancer

Gemini

Taurus

Aries

Orion

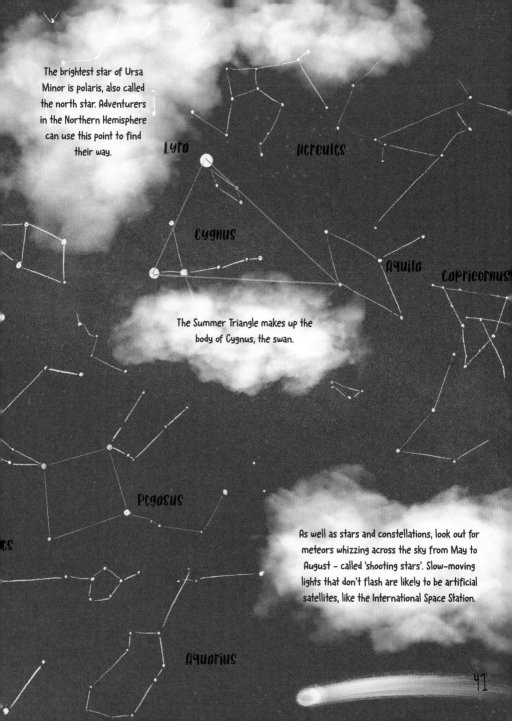

The brightest star of Ursa Minor is polaris, also called the north star. Adventurers in the Northern Hemisphere can use this point to find their way.

Lyra

Hercules

Cygnus

Aquila

Capricornus

The Summer Triangle makes up the body of Cygnus, the swan.

Pegasus

As well as stars and constellations, look out for meteors whizzing across the sky from May to August - called 'shooting stars'. Slow-moving lights that don't flash are likely to be artificial satellites, like the International Space Station.

Aquarius

41

Garden Flowers Guide

There are over 250,000 different flowers in the world! Though it would take a long time to memorize all their names, you can make a start by learning some common garden flowers with this guide.

Bluebell

Do not pick plants without permission, especially wild flowers.

Crocus

These bell-shaped flowers can be found in woodlands in spring.

Daffodil

Carnation

Daisy

Dahlia

Be careful –
some plants and
flowers are poisonous,
like Foxglove, or can
irritate the skin.

Foxgloves have
pretty pastel
flowers but their
leaves are poisonous!

Foxglove

Forget-me-not

Hyacinth

Freesia

43

Lavender

Lupin

Jasmine

Lily

Bee Orchid

Moth Orchid

Some orchids
tempt in pollinators
by producing flowers
that resemble female insects,
and have a scent like
them, too!

Peony

Poppy

Bowl-shaped,
white, cream, pink,
yellow or red flowers,
peonies bloom briefly in
late spring or early
summer.

Rose

Tulips

Sunflower

45

Grow your own

Spring Flowers

Spring flowers need to be planted in the autumn in order to bloom when the weather gets warm again in March, April and May.

You will need:

- a selection of spring bulbs, such as daffodils or tulips
- patch of soil (or a plant pot filled with soil if you don't have much outside space)
- trowel
- plant markers or recycled ice-lolly sticks
- felt-tip pen
- watering can

Always ask an adult for help when gardening. Remember, you'll also need their permission first.

How to plant bulbs:

1. Dig a hole two to three times the depth of the bulb you want to plant, and twice as wide.

2. Sit the bulb in the bottom of the hold, and if it has a point, make sure this is facing upward.

3. Replace the soil around the bulb and pat it down gently. Careful not to tread on the area, or you might damage the bulb!

4. Write the name of the flower on a plant marker or recycled ice-lolly stick and push it into the soil nearby, so you don't forget what's planted there.

5. Give the soil a sprinkle of water, unless it is already moist.

6. Watch your flowers bloom in springtime!

Tulips

Bird Spotting Guide

You don't need to make any special trips to go bird watching – feathered friends can be found all around us, though they can sometimes be hard to spot! Which ones can you find?

Be careful not to disturb birds or their nests.

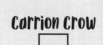

Blackbird ☐

Carrion Crow ☐

Blue Tit ☐

European Magpie ☐

Goldfinch

☐

Great Tit

☐

Great Spotted Woodpecker

☐

Male and female woodpeckers work together to peck nest cavities. You can often hear the distinctive 'tok-tok-tok' of their drumming in spring.

Grey Heron

☐

House Martin

☐

49

Jay

☐

You'll find different birds in different places but no matter where you go, always make sure you have permission to be outside and that the spot you choose is safe.

House Sparrow

☐

Robin

☐

Robins sing all year round – at night, they will even sing beside street lights.

Tawny Owl

☐

These nocturnal birds can fly almost silently due to the special shape and texture of their feathers. With their distinctive hooting call, tawny owls are more often heard than seen.

50

Starling ☐

Swift ☐

Song Thrush ☐

Wood Pigeon ☐

Wren ☐

51

Make a

Bird Feeder

Create a feeder to help attract birds to your garden
and feed hungry beaks when food is scarce.

You will need:

Bird seed often contains nuts, so avoid this activity if you have a nut allergy.

- empty milk carton or plastic drinks bottle
- scissors
- dowel or stick
- bird seed
- string

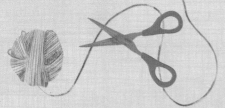

2. Use the tip of your scissors to make a small hole on opposite sides of the bottle, below the new opening. Ask an adult to help if you need. Push the dowel or stick through but leave it poking out on each side for a perch.

3. Make sure the inside of your feeder is clean and dry. Pour in some bird seed, so it fills the container up to the bottom of your hole.

1. Cut a round 10 cm hole in the side of your milk carton or drinks bottle.

4. Loop the string round the neck of the carton or bottle. Ask a grown-up to tie it securely to a tree in your garden or out of a window.

Be careful when using scissors. Make sure there is a grown-up around to help with this activity.

53

Animal SpOtting Guide

Some of these shy creatures are likely to be regular visitors to your garden or local park, but aren't always so keen on being seen!

Amphibians

Move slowly and try to make as little noise as possible when watching wildlife. Also do not touch or handle wild animals as that will scare or harm them.

☐ Newt

Species include: smooth newt, great crested newt, palmate newt
Where to look: in and around ponds

☐ Toad

Species include: common toad (pictured), natterjack
Where to look: around ponds

☐ Frog

Species include: common frog (pictured), pool frog
Where to look: in and around ponds

54

Reptiles

 Lizard

Species include: common lizard (pictured), sand lizard

Where to look: grasslands and sandy heathland on sunny days

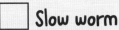 **Slow worm**

Where to look: woodland edges, compost heaps

Snake

Species include: Smooth snake (pictured), grass snake, adder

Where to look: grassland for grass snakes, heathland or woodland for adders and smooth snakes

Adders are Britain's only venomous snake.

Mammals

☐ **Red Fox**

Where to look: a wide range of habitats, including farmland, woodlands and urban areas. Foxes are nocturnal, so your best chance of spotting them is at night-time

☐ **Badger**

Where to look: woodlands at dusk, when badger families come out of their setts to forage

☐ **Mouse**

Species include: wood mouse (pictured), house mouse, harvest mouse

Where to look: mice make their homes in all sorts of habitats, including woodlands, farmland, and houses

☐ **Rat**

Species include: brown rat (pictured), black rat

Where to look: rats often live near water and are excellent swimmers

☐ **Hedgehog**

Where to look: hedgehogs hibernate in winter, so your best chance of spotting one is on warm nights in spring and summer when they come out to forage in gardens after dark

☐ **Squirrel**

Species include: red squirrel (pictured), grey squirrel

Where to look: grey squirrels can often be spotted in parks, gardens and woodlands, but red squirrels are much rarer

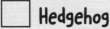

☐ **Bat**

Species include: common pipistrelle (pictured), brown long-eared bat, Brandt's bat

Where to look: in the sky around sunrise and sunset

Become a Wildlife Detective

Even if you don't see any wildlife, the signs that creatures have visited an area are easy to spot for adventurers who know where to look.

- Scrapings and scratchings on tree bark could signal that deer are nearby and have rubbed at the trees with their antlers.

- Droppings are a sure sign that creatures have passed through an area. If they look moist, they are probably quite fresh, but if they are faded and dry, they are probably a few days old.

- Pellets at the base of tree trunks may indicate that owls are nesting above. Pellets look a bit like droppings, but they are actually chunks of regurgitated food that the owl couldn't digest.

Dawn and dusk are the best times to see wild animals, as this is often when they are at their most active as they set out in search of food.

Create a Wildlife Hide

Watching wildlife is much easier if the wildlife doesn't spot you first and scarper! Create a hide to spy on creatures in their natural habitats.

Pick somewhere sheltered

Choose a spot where you have a good view of the surrounding area, but are partially hidden, such as behind a tree trunk. Use sticks and dark-covered tarpaulin or old bedsheets to make a simple shelter. You could try the teepee on pages 28–29.

Keep it camouflaged

Wear clothing that blends in with the area and cover your hide with branches so that passing wildlife won't spot it.

Ask an adult for their permission first before you try this activity..

Keep the noise down

You'll need to be patient in order to spot wildlife. You could take a good book, or some paper and pens for drawing, to keep yourself entertained while you wait.

Go Pond Dipping

All sorts of creatures make their homes in ponds. Discover what's lurking beneath the water by going on a pond-dipping adventure.

You will need:

It's important to stay safe when you are near water. Make sure an adult is there to supervise you.

- old clothes and wellies

- a long-handled net

- a light coloured plastic tray or empty tub, like an empty clean butter tub

1. With a grown up, go out to your garden pond. Wear old clothes and wellies. If you don't have a pond, ask your grown-up if there are any ponds in your area that allow pond dipping.

2. Half fill your tub or tray with pond water.

3. Swirl your net around the pond's surface gently, then empty it into your tub or tray. What can you spot? Use the guide on pages 54–55 to identify some of the most common pond-dwellers.

4. Swirl the net around a few more times in different areas of the pond, asking a grown-up to take over if it's hard to reach.

5. When you've finished pond dipping, tip the contents of the tub back into the water carefully.

Avoid touching the pond minibeasts and always wash your hands after going pond dipping!

Minibeast Spotting Guide

Some of these incredible insects like to wriggle and crawl around your garden or local park. How many can you spot on your outdoor adventures?

Insects have six legs. Their bodies are divided into three parts – a head, a thorax and an abdomen.

☐ Honeybee

☐ Garden a

Bees visit flowers to collect nectar and pollen, which they use as food for themselves and the larvae in their hives or nests. By moving from flower to flower, they are vital pollinators of many garden and wild flowers.

☐ Social wasp

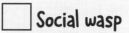

☐ White-tailed bumblebee

Beetles are a sub-group of insects. They have protective wing cases and mouth parts called mandibles.

☐ Ladybird

There are more than 40 species of ladybird in Britain.

☐ Rose Chafer

☐ Monarch butterfly

Monarch butterflies are found in North America. They are well-known for their seasonal migration. Millions of monarchs migrate from the United States and Canada south to California and Mexico for the winter.

☐ Bluebottle fly

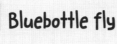

☐ Hawk moth

The lifecycle of an insect is egg - larva - pupa- adult or egg-nymph-adult. Insects, like butterflies, true flies and beetles , undergo complete metamorphosis, meaning they transform so dramatically in a pupal stage that the adult form doesn't resemble the larva.

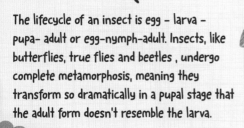

☐ Harvestman

Arachnids have eight legs, they spin silk from their abdomens and most inject digesting fluid into their prey before sucking up the insides like soup!

☐ Garden snail

Molluscs have soft bodies and most grow shells for protection. Snails and slugs are molluscs.

☐ Woodlouse

Crabs and lobsters are the most famous members of the crustacean family, but land-dwelling woodlice also fall into this category.

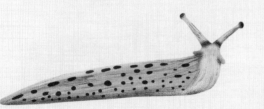

☐ Great grey slug

Snails are familiar animals that can cause a lot of damage in the garden, eating holes in leaves, stems and flowers.

☐ **Large black slug**

☐ **Brown centipede**

Myriapods are a distinctive group of invertebrates with lots and lots of legs! Centipedes and millipedes are myriapods. Centipedes have one pair of legs per body segment, while millipedes have two pairs.

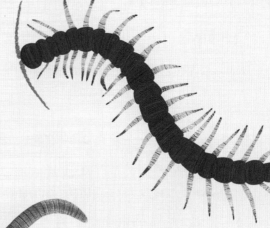

☐ **Earthworm**

Annelids have soft bodies made up of numerous segments. Earthworms and leeches are both annelids.

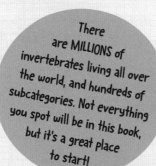

There are MILLIONS of invertebrates living all over the world, and hundreds of subcategories. Not everything you spot will be in this book, but it's a great place to start!

Bugs in the Garden

You share your garden with many amazing creatures. Discover some of the incredible insects and creepy crawlies that are great for your garden.

This page will tell you about the important jobs minibeasts do in the garden. Some insects help to get rid off damaging pests by eating them or even laying eggs inside them. Pollinating insects help your plants and flowers grow. Others perform the vital task of breaking down decaying material to help the soil. Every creature has an important role in our world, and here a just a few to get you started.

Ladybirds

Many Ladybirds are predatory on aphids and other insects, so they can help with your garden pests.

Spiders

Many varieties of spiders spin elaborate webs up to 60 centimetres (2 feet) wide, and lie in wait for unsuspecting garden invaders to become entangled in the sticky threads.

Beetles

The Rose chafer is often seen on flowers in the garden, and is sometimes considered a pest for munching its way through plants. However, many beetles feed on dead and decaying matter and recycle its nutrients - a helpful addition to any compost heap.

Social wasp

You might be scared of wasps because of their sting, but they're also helping in your garden. Wasps hunts caterpillars and other insects in summer to feed their grubs.

Bees

Bees are familiar and much-loved insects that pollinate our crops and wildflowers. As bees visit plants seeking food, pollen catches on their bodies and passes between plants, fertilising them. Butterflies and hoverflies are also great pollinators.

Centipedes and millipedes

Centipedes are not garden pests at all. They do not attack plants, feeding instead on small soil animals and slugs. Millipedes feed mainly on decaying plant material, however they can also damage seedlings and bedding plants, such as peas, beans and tomatoes.

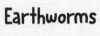

Earthworms

Earthworms offer many benefits from their activity in the soil: increased nutrient availability, better drainage, and a more stable soil structure, all of which can help improve plant growth in your garden.

Make a

Bug Hotel

Some of these shy creatures are likely to be regular visitors to your garden or local park, but aren't always so keen on being seen!

You will need:

- scissors
- large juice carton or plastic bottle, washed and dried
- straw
- natural materials, including moss, leaves, pinecones (optional), bark, twigs

1. Cut a large window out of your carton of plastic bottle, almost the whole height and width of one side.

2. Poke layers of natural materials into the bottle so visiting bugs will have lots of different layers to explore.

Ask an adult to help you with the scissors in this activity.

3. Once you've filled up your hotel, find somewhere in your garden or on a balcony or an outside windowsill to put it.

4. Check on your hotel every few days to see if any insects are on a visit. Why not keep a guestbook of who comes to stay?

69

Welcome Wildlife

Help protect habitats and make your green space a haven for wildlife by providing places to forage, nest and rear their young.

Try not to use pestic
sprays in your garde
– a happy garden will h
creatures in balance wi
each other.

Piles of dead leaves, trimmings and rotting wood provide lots of hidey-holes for beetles and other invertebrates to explore.

Compost heaps can provide safe places for creatures like hedgehogs and slow worms. Find out how to make one on the next page!

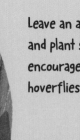

Leave an area of lawn uncut and plant some wildflowers to encourage bees, butterflies and hoverflies to visit.

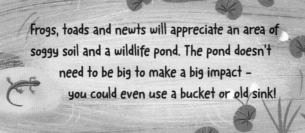

Frogs, toads and newts will appreciate an area of soggy soil and a wildlife pond. The pond doesn't need to be big to make a big impact – you could even use a bucket or old sink!

Bird boxes, hedgehog homes and bug hotels are also great ways of welcoming wildlife that might be struggling to find somewhere safe to live or hibernate over the winter.

A shallow birdbath full of clean water won't just provide a drink for thirsty birds. If you place a few large pebbles as stepping stones, you might spot bees and butterflies stopping for a sip, too, although British species don't often do this.

Make your Own Compost

Garden compost is full of nutrients that help plants grow and compost heaps provide habitats for lots of garden wildlife. Make your own super-soil from kitchen and garden waste.

Metal mesh is better for the environment. Plastic netting cannot be recycled.

You will need:

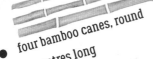

- four bamboo canes, round 1.5 metres long

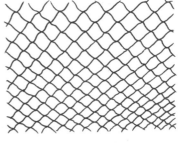

- metal mesh (chicken wire) or plastic netting

- tape measure or measuring sticks

- watering can

- thin gardening wire, cut into ten 8 cm lengths

1. Push one bamboo cane firmly into the ground. This will be your first corner.

2. Using the tape measure or measuring sticks, create a 1 x 1 m square with a cane at each corner and firmly push them into position.

3. Carefully unroll the mesh or netting and slowly walk around the square, wrapping the four canes until they are completely enclosed.

4. Push the garden wire through the mesh, around each cane, and twist the ends tightly to secure them in place. Use at least two pieces of wire per cane – one near the top and one near the bottom. On the last cane, make sure the wire feeds through both layers of overlapped mesh. Your compost bin is ready to use!

Metal mesh and wire can be sharp. Ask an adult for help with this activity.

5. Gather up dead leaves, organic food waste (like vegetable ends and peelings) along with any garden trimmings and pile them inside your compost bin. Sprinkle some water on top, as this will help the leaves to rot and form compost more quickly.

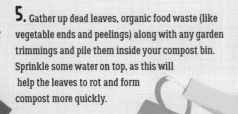

6. Composting takes a bit of patience, but in around a year, the pile should have formed a dark, crumbly material – perfect for helping new plants to grow!

Grow your Own Herbs

Herbs are fragrant and tasty plants that give food fantastic flavour. It's easy to grow your own – you don't even need plant pots, as herbs grow just as well in recycled containers.

You will need:

- a few recycled containers, washed and dried, such as glass jars, yoghurt pots or drinks cartons with the top snipped off
- potting compost
- herb seeds like basil, coriander and mint
- permanent marker
- water

1. Fill your containers with potting compost and plant your herb seeds as per the packet instructions. Write the name of the herb you've planted on the outside of the container in permanent marker.

2. Sprinkle over water so the soil is damp, but not too soggy, then put your herb pots somewhere warm and bright (though not in direct sunlight).

Mint

3. Once your herbs have sprouted, usually in one to two weeks, you can move them to a sunnier spot, like a windowsill.

4. In a couple of months, your herbs should be ready to harvest. Try adding different herbs to your dinner and see which is your favourite!

Basil

Coriander

Mint

Planting Potatoes

Not only is homegrown food delicious, it's good for the planet, too. If you have a large back garden, you could create a vegetable patch in a sunny spot. But it's easy to grow potatoes in sack even if you only have a tiny bit of outdoor space. This is a fun activity for spring.

You will need:

- thick potato peelings with eyes (little sprouts)
- a large pot or a recycled carrier bag (such as a 'bag for life') or potato sack
- compost
- scissors
- small spade or trowel

If you're using a recycled carrier bag, rather than a potato sack, snip a few tiny holes in the bottom for wate to drain through before fillin with compost..

1. Fill your bag or sack half full with compost.

2. Pick some potato peelings that have a small sprout on them, called a potato eye.

3. Place the peelings in soil with the eyes facing up. Sprinkle over another layer of compost so the peelings are well covered.

4. Place the bag or sack in a sunny spot, close to a house wall for shelter. Water whenever the soil feels dry. Sprinkle over some more compost when leaves start to show.

5. In around twelve to fourteen weeks, your delicious potatoes should be ready to harvest!

Grow Your Own Tomatoes

Tomatoes taste best picked straight off the vine. They love sunny weather and can be grown in the greenhouse or outside in the summer.

You will need:

- large yoghurt pots (washed and dried) or small plant pots
- potting compost
- tomato seeds
- water
- trowel

1. Fill your yoghurt or plant pots with potting compost and tap them on a flat surface so the soil is level.

2. Wet the compost with some tap water and let it drain. Then gently press two or three tomato seeds into the pots, then cover with more compost.

3. Leave the pots on a warm, sunny windowsill to sprout.

Tomatoes

4. Once your tomatoes have started to grow, carefully move the sprouting seeds so there is just one plant per pot.

Tomatoes

Tomatoes

Tomatoes

5. In late spring, move your tomatoes outside. You can grow them in a large pot or growbag or plant them into the ground if you have a garden. Wait until the first flowers have formed, then dig a hole at least twice as wide as the pot and transfer your tomato plant into the ground. Use a watering can to give your plant a drink whenever the compost or soil is dry.

When growing tomatoes, remove the side shoots regularly. Side shoots grow where the base of the leaf joins the main stem. If the packet describes your tomato as a 'bush' type there is no need to do any pinching!

77

Rainbow
Salad Recipe

Brighten up a picnic with this crunchy salad recipe. You could even grow your own ingredients and experiment with different flavour and colour combinations.

You want your salad to have as many different colours as possible! Pick bright, healthy ingredients like:

- peppers or tomatoes (red)
- carrots or cooked butternut squash (orange)
- sweetcorn or peach slices (yellow)

- lettuce, cucumber, avocado or sugar snap peas (green)
- beetroot, red onion or cabbage (purple)

1. Wash your ingredients well and set them aside to dry for a few minutes or pat them dry with a clean tea towel.

2. Carefully chop the ingredients into chunks so they are roughly the same size.

3. Mix your salad together in a bowl or arrange each of the ingredients side-by-side in the shape of a rainbow.

4. Serve up your rainbow salad with a smile!

Ask an adult to help you with this activity.

Picnic Party

Next time there's a sunny day, gather some friends and head out on an adventure to find the perfect picnic spot.

Pack a blanket, or a few old towels, and lay them out in a shady, flat area.

Keep your snacks in sealed cont[ainers] when you're not eating, to avoi[d your] picnic being invaded by wasps an[d]

After your picnic is finished, make sure you take home any rubbish, and leave the spot just as you found it.

Fill these plates with ideas for your dream picnic spread!

Ask all your friends to bring a food item – make sure everybody agrees what they're bringing first. You could try making the rainbow salad from the previous page.

Once everybody's eaten, you could play some outdoor games – there are some ideas on pages 20–23!

Wellie Planters

Brighten up your garden by transforming worn-out wellies in wonderful planters. What will you grow inside?

You will need:

- old wellington boots
- a sharp knife or electric drill (and a grown-up to use it!)
- some pebbles
- potting compost
- some seeds, bulbs or shrubs for planting

Ask an adult to help you with this activity.

Potting Compost

1. Ask a grown-up to make some drainage holes in the bottom of the wellies using a knife or electric drill.

2. Put a layer of pebbles in the bottom of your boots (this will also help the water drain through).

3. Add potting compost until the boots are around three-quarters full. Plant your seeds, bulbs or shrubs according to their instructions and sprinkle over some more compost and a little water.

4. Put in a sunny spot and water the wellies whenever the soil feels dry.

There's plenty of fun to be had outside, even if it's raining. From splashing in puddles to searching for wet-weather-loving wildlife. But if you don't fancy going out in the rain, you can bring nature inside, too!

Leaf-print Wrapping Paper

You will need:

- poster paints
- old plates
- paint brushes
- a roll of brown paper
- a selection of leaves

1. Squeeze some paint out onto each of the plates (one colour per plate) and mix it around with a paint brush.

2. Choose a leaf and carefully press it onto the plate, so it's covered in a thin layer of paint.

3. Press your painted leaf onto the brown paper. Repeat this, pressing it back into the paint when needed, so you start to build up a pattern.

4. Take another leaf and press it into some different-coloured paint. Continue building up your design until you're happy with your leaf-print paper!

5. Once the paint is dry, you could use it to wr presents, or even put a section in a frame to brighten up a wall of yo bedroom

Nature noughts and crosses

You will need:

- white poster paint
- a paint brush
- ten smooth pebbles or conkers of roughly equal size
- four sticks of roughly equal length

Paint

1. Using your white paint, draw 'O's on five of your pebbles or conkers, and 'X's on the other five. Leave to dry.

2. Arrange your sticks into a grid, with two vertical and two horizontal, so you have three squares across and three down. If you like, you could collect four more sticks to mark the edges of the grid.

3. With a friend, take it in turns putting a nought or a cross into a grid square. Whoever gets three in a row first, either vertically, horizontally, or diagonally, wins!

My Outdoor Adventure Diary

Use these pages to write about all your outdoor adventures! Keep notes of any seeds or bulbs you plant, any wildlife you spot and any exciting nature trips you go on! You could stick in some of your own drawings or pictures, too.

Glossary

bacteria Tiny organisms that live on, in and around most living and non-living things. Some can be harmful and cause disease.

bark The outer layer of a tree's trunk.

bloom To produce a flower.

bulb A round plant bud that begins to grow underground.

compass A tool that uses magnetised needles to show the direction of magnetic north. It helps users to work out the direction in which they need to go.

compost A type of soil, good for growing plants in. Garden compost for adding to soil is made from a mixture of rotting matter, such as leaves, kitchen scraps and grass. Potting compost is good for growing plants in pots in.

coniferous Trees that produce cones – many keep their leaves all year round, such as pine trees and fir trees.

constellation A group of stars that form a recognized pattern. Scientists have identified 88 constellations in the night sky.

deciduous Plants and trees that lose their leaves at certain times of the year, such as oak trees and maple trees.

decompose To break down, decay and become rotten.

edible Something that can be eaten.

evergreen Plants and trees that keep their leaves all year round, such as holly and palms.

floret A small flower, often one that makes up part of a bigger flowerhead.

flower The part of a plant that blooms, has petals and makes fruits or seeds.

forage To search for food.

germinate When a seed begins to sprout.

germs Very small organisms or bugs that often causes diseases.

harvest Collecting seeds or picking fruits, vegetables or other edible plants.

herb A plant which is used to flavour food.

hygiene Anything you do to keep yourself and your surroundings clean and healthy.

nectar A sugary liquid in flowers that plants use to attract pollinating animals.

nocturnal animals Creatures that are active at night and sleep during the day.

poisonous Something that will make you ill or even kill you if you eat it.

pollen Fine grains produced by the male parts of flowers that combine with the female parts of plants to produce seeds.

pollination The process where pollen is moved from a male part to a female part of a plant, or between plants, so the plant can produce seeds.

pollinator Animals that cause pollination to happen by transferring pollen, such as bees, bats and birds. Some plants are pollinated by the wind.

root The part of the plant which gives it support by attaching it to the ground. The roots also carry water and nutrients from the soil to the rest of the plant.

scale The ratio between real life sizes and how many times something has been shrunk to fit it on the map.

seed A small part of a plant from which new plants grow.

seedling A young plant that has developed from a seed.

sow To plant seeds.

stem The stalk of a plant.

track pattern A series of tracks that shows an animal's steps and movements. Different animals move across the ground in lots of different ways, such as crawling, waddling and galloping.

trowel A small garden tool with a pointed scoop.

weed A plant that gardeners want to pull up because it is pushing out its neighbouring plants or growing in the wrong place.

Index